M000033938

Cat Haiku

Cat Haiku

Deborah Coates

with illustrations by Sheila Moxley

C
CENTURY

CENTURY · LONDON

Published by Century in 2001

1 3 5 7 9 10 8 6 4 2

Copyright © Deborah Coates 2001
Illustrations © Sheila Moxley 2001 [sheilamoxley.com]
Designed by Juliet Rowley

First published in the United Kingdom by 2001 by Century
The Random House Group Limited
20 Vauxhall Bridge Road, London SW1V 2SA

Random House Australia (Pty) Limited
20 Alfred Street, Milsons Point, Sydney,
New South Wales 2061, Australia

Random House New Zealand Limited
18 Poland Road, Glenfield,
Auckland 10, New Zealand

Random House South Africa (Pty) Limited
Endulini, 5a Jubilee Road,
Parktown 2193, South Africa

The Random House Group Limited Reg. No. 954009

www.randomhouse.co.uk

A CIP catalogue record for this book
is available from the British Library

Papers used by Random House UK Limited are natural, recyclable products made from wood
grown in sustainable forests. The manufacturing processes conform to the environmental
regulations of the country of origin.

ISBN 0 7126 79537

Typeset in PixieFont and Garamond by MATS, Southend-on-Sea, Essex
Printed and bound in Denmark by Nørhaven A/S, Viborg

For Quinn,

the best godson in the world

Acknowledgements

My heartfelt thanks to:

. . . Sharon Gedan, who over the years has helped me put the pieces together more times than either of us probably wants to think about;

. . . my parents, who instilled in me a love of books so profound that I'm still amazed I stopped reading long enough to write one of my own;

. . . Jackie Matosian, who gave me the idea for *Cat Haiku*;

. . . my agent, Todd Keithley, and editor, Amy Einhorn, whose enthusiasm, interest, patience, and support made the mysteries of first-time book publication a joy;

. . . and most of all, my grandmother, who taught me how to laugh at life, and at myself.

I owe an enormous debt to you all.

Contents

Introduction 12

Socializing 16

Recreation 30

Home Decorating 43

Keeping Fit 54

Food and Drink 64

Under the Weather 74

Personal Issues 84

9

Contents

Repose 92

Ongoing Concerns 100

Small Amusements 110

Secret Pleasures 124

Things I Wonder About 134

The Differences between Us 144

Holidays 160

Not-So-Random Thoughts 172

Introduction

Some of you more inquisitive types are bound to ask,
'Why write a book of cat haiku?'

Good question. My thoughtful, reasoned response as
a woman of letters is . . . I have no idea. It just sort of happened
– probably because I like cats, and I also like haiku (and haiku,
by the way, for those of you who don't know, is a three-line,
unrhymed Japanese verse form of five, seven, and five syllables
respectively. So there.)

Really, though, I suppose I wrote *Cat Haiku* because cats seem
to think – and even communicate – in a haiku-like fashion.
And that's intriguing, and often funny:

Oh, good. You're home. I

Celebrate joyously with

A rousing ear-twitch.

See what I mean? Cats are, simply, the animal embodiment of haiku. Both are subtle, elegant, succinct; every nuance is fraught with meaning (however obscure that meaning may sometimes be, and believe me, it frequently is). You pay attention when you read haiku because you don't want to miss anything, and you pay attention when cats are around because you don't want to miss anything, either. There's no skimming with either one. (And if there is, especially with the latter, woe betide you.)

Also, both cats and haiku have staying power. Domestic cats have been around since the heyday of Ancient Egypt, and haiku dates from the seventeenth century or thereabouts.

I mean, we're talking *classics* here.

And who can argue with that?

Socializing

You may call it 'a

Lot of yowling'. I call it

Singing to my friends.

A cat friend visits.

I swat him anyway, just

For principle's sake.

I think that the new

Kitten makes a fine punching

Bag and trampoline

You are my best friend,

Person Allergic to Cats.

Let me shed on you.

I grope under the

Door with a splayed paw; I know

You're in there. Come out!

We meet outside; I

Startle. You're out of context;

Go back inside, please!

Visitors come. They

Coo over me. Ignoring

Them, I wash my rump.

Your friends seem nice: calm,

Attentive and kind. So when

Are they going home?

I hide under the

Bed. I don't want to be friends.

Take that child away!

There will be canine

Parts missing if that dog gets

Anywhere near me.

You want to cuddle;

I don't. No offence meant, but

Right now you bore me.

I yowl to the moon;

I am king of the night. Hear

Me and weep, Fluffy.

Recreation

To you, a water-

Filled sink. To me, a fish pond.

It just takes vision.

Surprise! I can jump

Through the newspaper while you

Are still reading it!

On safari, I

Prowl old shoes and sporting goods

In our junk closet.

Fresh catnip's no fun.

Now, some nice extremely dead mole –

That's good to roll in!

Paper clips, coins, an

Ice cube, you name it. I can

Slapshoot anything.

This ball is boring.

But if you had brought me a

Nice small frightened bird ... !

Styrofoam peanuts:

To you, packaging. To me,

Rodent substitutes.

Those little toy mice

Are dumb; bring me an injured

Lizard or something.

Look at it from my

Perspective: clean laundry is

Meant for prowling in.

Velcro-tab sneakers

Are dull. Shoelaces, now – those

Are fascinating.

Home Decorating

Is it not lovely

The way my fur wafts through the

Air when you pet me?

Au contraire; I think

The couch looks better with a

Few shredded cushions

I disagree with

You. I think cat hair dresses

The place up nicely.

I can't help it if

The curtain rod is not strong

Enough to hold me.

So I have done some

Flower arranging. I need

Roughage, too, you know.

I know you're mad, but

Just think: it takes planning to

Knock over a chair!

I leave sharp kibble

Bits where you'll step on them with

Your tender bare feet.

Voilà: grey paw prints

On the countertops. What an

Artistic statement!

Lamps are convenient

For trapping moths, but they do

Tip over a lot.

The scrunched-up throw rugs

Add a nice casual touch

Of welcome, don't they?

I fix one thing, you

Change it back. I just can't keep

Things nice around here.

Keeping Fit

I am a strong and

Adventurous cat. So I

Can't climb down. Big deal.

It's hard to explain:

Bare toes look just like small pink

Mice. Ergo, I pounce.

I leap for a bird

And miss. I pretend I was

Stretching, to fool you.

You don't get it: a

Scratching post is too easy.

Now, a chair leg – ah!

I'm not digging in

The carpet; I'm exploring

My Inner Kitten.

I stretch forward, then

Scrunch back. Pointing my paws is

Simply good form. See?

Studies have shown that

It is much easier to

Climb walls by moonlight.

It's hard to drink out

Of the toilet, but it's a

Personal challenge.

Biff! Crash! I bounce off

The walls. I'm not crazy, I'm

Self-actualised.

Food and Drink

Warning: I can't be

Trusted if fresh sushi is

Left unattended.

If this stuff is so

'Good and nutritious', then why

Don't you eat kibble?

You don't understand.

The water in the toilet

Tastes a LOT better.

How would you like it

If your food was dried into

Hard little brown bits?

If I were fed an

Occasional salad, I

Would never eat grass.

Hasn't anyone

Around here ever heard of

Something called wet food?

You like ethnic food –

So why shouldn't I sneak the

Dog's food when I can?

I'm not sure what this

Was when it was alive, but

Isn't it nice now?

You say chocolate

Is bad for cats, but I think

You are just greedy.

Under the Weather

If the vet took your

Temperature that way, I

Bet you'd complain, too.

I would have thought you'd

Thank me for getting sick where

You could not see it.

Poinck! I spit out the

Pill underneath the stove and

Watch you fish for it.

My stomach revolts:

A leaf, saliva, grass. A

Feline sushi plate.

It takes practice to

Sneeze medicine in your face.

I'm good at it, huh?

Driving to the vet

I MUST crouch underneath this

Nice safe gas pedal

Now we know: I should

Not eat sardines even if

It is my birthday.

You went away; I

Stayed at the vet's. Why should I

Acknowledge you now?

A truth we both know:

The cat carrier is not

'A fun place to play'!

Personal Issues

I don't make you lick

Yourself, so why must I be

Bathed with flea shampoo?

I wait for you to

Clean the rugs. Hack! Hack! Here: my

Best hairball to date.

You are wrong. There's no

Rule that says the litter must

Stay inside the box.

I like to pick at

My feet with my teeth; it's a

Cat thing. Let it go.

Yes, actually,

I am burying a moose

In the litter box!

Oops: another hair

Ball. Sorry; guess I'm having

A bad hair ball day.

Eyes closed, I lick and

Lick my fur. One gets into

The Zen of it all.

Repose

Sometimes my front legs

Keep walking while my back legs

Decide to lie down.

It's true: cats always

Know the most comfortable

Place. But you won't fit.

I don't like my bed.

I prefer your favourite

Chair. So you should move.

Yes, this broken-neck

Sleeping position is quite

Popular with us.

Sometimes when I sit

On your lap, I'm a kitten

Again. It will pass.

You read books; I like

To lie on top of them. We're

Both bibliophiles.

I sleep with one paw

Protecting my nose. You just

Can't be too careful.

Ongoing Concerns

I watch you use the

Vacuum cleaner but I still

Think it will eat me.

I figure if I

Stare at this door long enough,

You will let me out.

I hump my back in

Stiff disapproval. One day

I may tell you why.

I hate the garbage

Man. He's noisy and never

Spills anything good.

I sit in front of

The door. You open it; I

Stare. Nope. changed my mind.

I'm quiet; you're loud.

I want to play; you want to

Read. And so it goes.

I wasn't really

Waiting for you. No, I just

Happened to be here.

Delicately, I

Sniff your hand. You've been petting

A strange cat. Traitor!

Small Amusements

I lick your hand and

Watch you pretend to like it.

This amuses me.

Up in my cat tree

I watch you pass by. Growling,

I jump on your head.

Don't be so crabby.

I'm not 'biting your hair', I'm

Checking you for fleas.

I purr on your lap.

Then I decide I don't know

You. I scratch you hard.

I sit, nose to the

Wall, and stare at it. I know

You'll investigate.

You use dental floss.

So what's wrong with chewing on

Electrical cords?

I like to sniff at

Your feet till you feel odd and

Try to get away.

You call and I hear.

But I am a jungle cat

And will not answer.

I deign to play with

The string because you look so

Silly dragging it.

Sometimes when I'm bored

I hunch up and look ill just

To make you nervous.

I reach out a claw

And catch a thread in your best

Shirt. It snags; I yawn.

You have a nightmare.

I fling myself against the

Door to cheer you up.

Secret Pleasures

Give me one reason

Why in heaven's name I should

Not sleep in the sink.

I like it when you

Rub just inside my ears. You'd

Make a good Q-Tip.

When I'm pleased, I stick

Out the tip of my tongue. Hey,

We all do SOMEthing.

Poor you. Only your

Head fits on this expensive

Down pillow? How sad.

I like to rub my

Head against you. Affection?

Nope – my ears just itch.

So I like to stretch

Out with my rump in the air.

It's just a small quirk.

See? The car windshield

Does make an absolutely

Perfect slide for me.

It's nice when you scratch

Just above my nose; that's an

Acupressure point.

Things I Wonder About

THE MEANING OF LIFE

WHY ARE WE HERE VOL V

WHAT'S IT ALL ABOUT?

I want out. I want

In. Out. In. Out. In. Out. In.

Are you angry yet?

To help support us

I leave small dead things on the

Doormat. Want some mouse?

You're dashing to work

In the rain. I yawn and stretch —

Don't you just hate me?

You lie on the couch;

I walk on your stomach. Should

I rest here? Maybe.

Nonchalantly, I

Try to free my claw from your

Shirt. What's so funny?

You rush, and I weave

Between your legs. You curse. Why?

This is my Cat Dance.

Just because I wrecked

The house, you're talking about

Guitar strings? Calm down.

You wash your hands when

You touch my flea collar. Why

Should I wear it, then?

What does it feel like

To be big, hairless, tail-less,

And pink? Bad, I'll bet.

The Differences Between Us

Now, wait a minute.

Me, wear a ribbon? You have

Got to be kidding.

I close my second

Eyelids a lot, just because

You don't have any.

You may have those odd

'Opposable thumbs', but I

Can talk with my tail.

I land on my feet

For the same reason you walk

Upright: I can. Hah!

You get a massage,

I roll in the dirt. Both are

Relaxing, aren't they?

Come on, admit it.

Don't you sometimes wish you had

Sharp little fangs, too?

You play cards; I like

To creep inside paper bags.

To each their own, huh?

Hey, if I wanted

To walk on the end of a

Leash, I'd be a dog!

You stomp around and

Yell; I lash my tail. There are

Other ways to swear.

Okay, so you blow

Your nose; I rub mine with a

Paw. Who looks cuter?

You do puzzles; I

Unwind viscera from dead

Prey. Hobbies differ.

You laugh, but I know

You wish your yawns swallowed up

Your entire face, too.

You must love this thing

Called 'work' since you go there so

Much. I'd rather nap.

You mean that when you're

Happy, all you can do is

Hum? That's pathetic.

Holidays

A tree to climb, light

Cords to bite, presents to prowl.

I love Christmastime.

You ignore it, but

I'd like to help that groundhog

See his old shadow!

Valentine's Day. Humpf.

I never see candy or

Cards coming my way.

Next St. Patrick's Day,

I'll turn something of yours green.

And it won't be food.

Ah, Easter: eggs and

Plastic grass. Now if I could

Just find that Bunny...

There's Mother's Day and

Father's Day, but no Cat Day.

Someone's head should roll.

Fireworks pop until

My eyes do, too. A pox on

Independence Day!

I won't help with the

Candles, but your birthday cake

Looks quite intriguing ...

Repeatedly, our

Door opens to loud children.

I loathe Halloween.

Thanksgiving: there are

No words. A dead bird bigger

Than I am, and cooked!

New Year's Eve is nice

If you're crazy. Me, I stay

Under the sofa.

Cats were revered in

Ancient Egypt. I think we

Should reclaim the past.

I love pantyhose.

But only when you have just

Put them on for work.

'There's more than one way

To skin a cat' – what sadist

Thought that one up, huh?

If you could see in

The dark like I can, you'd go

Crazy sometimes, too.

The Cat's Credo: 'All

Creatures Smaller Than You Are

Must Be Played to Death.'

There is no one as

Dignified as we cats; I

Think it's the whiskers.

I know I look odd

When I lie on my back, but

Guess what: you do, too.

A cat getting your

Tongue is impossible: you

Guys are way too tall.

No matter what you

Give me, I'll shake it in my

Mouth and break its neck.

You say 'It's raining

Cats and dogs.' I wonder what

You've been ingesting.

Please bear in mind that

You're part of my entourage,

And not vice versa.

A bit of advice:

Purring is just a decoy.

Trust me on this one.

Curiosity

May kill us cats, but hey – there

Are worse ways to go!

I feel no need to

Accomplish things. I exist;

That's triumph enough.

About the Author

Deborah Coates is a chronically amused and frequently

perplexed baby boomer who lives in Los Angeles

with her two cats, Pinch and Pippin. A native Southern

Californian, she is addicted to reading and international travel,

and would spend the rest of her days in jeans and Hawaiian

shirts if it were left up to her.

Got a cat haiku? Or other comments (preferably complimentary, but whatever)? Send 'em along to:

cathaiku@hotmail.com

They will be eagerly read and cheerfully responded to –
or at least the nice ones will be.